MW01174991

DISCOVERING CEREALS

Contents

written by
Angela Lucas

designed and
illustrated by
Susannah Bradley

YOUNG LIBRARY

First published in 1993 by
Young Library Ltd
3 The Old Brushworks
56 Pickwick Road
Corsham, Wiltshire SN13 9BX
England

ISBN 1 85429 013 4

Printed in Hong Kong

Goodness from Grass

How much grass do you eat? None, you think? Well, you may not GRAZE like a sheep, but when you eat bread or rice you do eat a kind of grass.

Bread is made from wheat. It is the most important food for almost half the people in the world. Rice is the most important for the other half. Maize is widely eaten too, but more as a food for cattle, pigs, and other animals.

Rice, wheat, and maize are all kinds of grass. Thousands of years ago they grew wild. People

The main use of wheat is to make bread. How many kinds of loaf can you see here?

found the GRAINS were good to eat so they began to grow them as CROPS.

Wheat, rice, and maize are known as 'cereal' crops. There are six others – barley, rye, oats, sorghum, millet, and triticale. But this book is about the three most important ones.

About half the cultivated land in the world has cereals growing on it. Wheat, rice, and maize supply two-thirds of the world's seed crops.

Wheat is ground into FLOUR. Flour is used to make bread. There are many kinds of bread – white and brown loaves, baguettes, chapattis, pitta bread, rolls, and so on. Then there are all the cakes, biscuits, pastries, and pizzas we enjoy – they are made of flour too. Macaroni, spaghetti, noodles, and other PASTAS are all made from wheat flour.

3

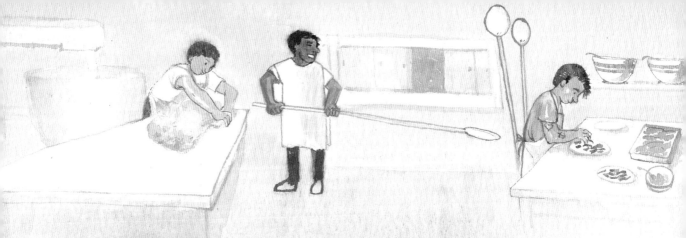

Most of the rice you eat is with meat or
vegetables. We use long-grained rice or medium-
grained rice for those dishes. In puddings we use
short-grained rice. In poor countries rice is eaten
mainly by itself. If you look at the supermarket
shelves you will discover where the different
types of rice come from.

We have many uses for cereal crops. Breakfast
cereals is one favourite way of eating them. If you

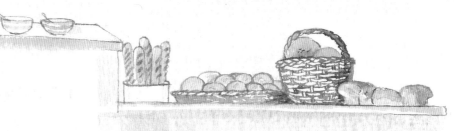

enjoy corn-on-the-cob, or popcorn, you are
eating maize. Cereals are also used to make
semolina and custard powder. Alcoholic drinks
are made from rice, wheat, and barley. Maize is

At the Monza Grand Prix, Italian mechanics snatch a few minutes' break for a spaghetti lunch.

used to feed farm animals in winter when grass will not grow.

Sometimes the crop will fail. Too much or too little rain ruins wheat. Rice dies in a drought. Birds and locusts feed on ripening grain. Maggots called stemborers eat the inside of rice stalks.

We, who live in rich countries, have many different foods to eat. But in some countries one of the cereal crops is the only food poor people have. In parts of Asia and Africa people die every year because that one food fails to grow.

Wheat

Wheat will grow almost anywhere in the world. It covers more land than any other crop. It grows below sea-level and in mountains of 3,000 metres. It will stand great heat or little heat, much rain and very little rain. It grows best, however, where the winter is chilly and the summer is warm and wet, but not *too* wet. The map on pages 12/13

After ploughing, and before planting, a wheat field must be harrowed to make it smooth.

will show you which countries are best for
wheat-growing.

Most of the biggest wheat growers are countries
where it did not grow at all 500 years ago! Those
are the United States, Canada, Australia, and
Argentina. In Australia half of all the land used for
crops has wheat on it. Wheat is an important crop
even in countries which grow a lot of rice. India
grows almost as much wheat as rice. In northern
China, where rice cannot grow, wheat is the
main food.

In autumn the farmer prepares the land. To
loosen the earth he pulls a plough behind his
powerful tractor. The plough turns the soil in
clean-cut furrows. Then he uses a harrow and
roller to make it smooth and firm. A drill drops
the seed grains in straight lines and covers them
up with earth. The most modern machines do all
these jobs at once.

As the crop grows, the farmer spreads fertilizer

to feed the plants. He sprays the fields to kill weeds, pests, and diseases.

The summer sun ripens the grain. The growing wheat becomes a plant as tall as your chest. On each stem dozens of new grains form and ripen.

The farmer drives his COMBINE HARVESTER across the fields. The fields might be so big that he cannot see to the end of them. In front of him the cutting bar cuts off the wheat just above ground level. It passes through the thresher, which separates the grain from the stalk. The CHAFF blows away. The grain pours out into a trailer.

The golden grain is taken away to be stored in an ELEVATOR. Warm air is blown through to dry it, otherwise it might turn mouldy.

A combine harvester advances towards the camera in this Western Australia wheatfield.

Some of the grain will be saved, to plant for next year's crop. All the rest is sent to be ground into flour. You can read about this in the last chapter.

In some countries the farmers are poor. They could not possibly afford machinery to do all this work. They have a plough pulled by one or two oxen. All the other jobs are done with hand tools.

Rice

Rice is the main food for at least a third of the people on earth. In parts of south-east Asia it is not just the main food, but the only food, for huge numbers of people. For them, food *means* rice.

Rice grows best in very hot and rainy places. Look at the map on pages 12/13 and you will see that most of the rice countries are in the tropics.

Many of the world's rice farmers are poor. They have only a small piece of land and very simple tools. They grow their crops on flat land beside rivers and streams. They call the fields PADDIES.

Rice needs to be flooded as it grows. Low earth walls surround the paddies. Water channels criss-cross them. Through these channels the farmer lets in the water.

In Taiwan a farmer prepares his rice beds with a roto-tiller. The fields will remain flooded until the rice is full-grown.

Rice is grown on hillsides too. The farmer cuts the hillside into flat terraces a bit like a flight of stairs. Each terraced paddy is watered by the overflow from the one above.

First, while the paddy is still dry, the farmer ploughs and flattens the earth. His plough is probably pulled by a buffalo. Meanwhile the rice grains are growing in the nursery bed.

Later, with their feet and hands in the muddy water, the farmer and his family set out the

The countries which grow most wheat, rice, and maize

Wheat
- Ukraine (1)
- China (2)
- United States (3)
- India (4)
- Canada (5)
- Argentina (6)
- Turkey (7)
- Australia (8)
- Pakistan (9)

Rice
- China (2)
- India (4)
- Indonesia (10)
- Bangladesh (11)
- Burma (12)
- Japan (13)
- Thailand (14)
- United States (3)

Maize
- United States (3)
- China (2)
- Brazil (15)
- Mexico (16)
- Rumania (17)
- Argentina (6)

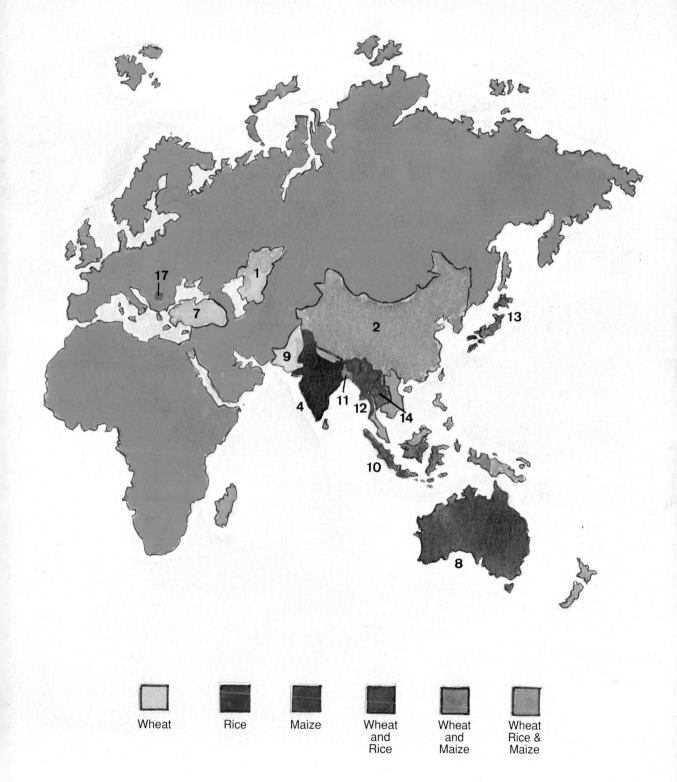

Wheat | Rice | Maize | Wheat and Rice | Wheat and Maize | Wheat Rice & Maize

young plants in neat rows. Little by little, as the crop grows, the farmer floods the paddy deeper. When the plants are about 80 centimetres high, and have turned from green to yellow, the farmer drains the paddy. For a few weeks the rice

Rice and maize are two of the crops to be seen in these terraced fields in Japan.

grows on dry land. Then the farmer and his family cut the stalks with knives. They lay the cut rice in the fields to dry. Then they carry it home in bundles. They beat it to separate the grain from the stalks.

The grain is stored in pots, baskets, or sacks, away from rats and mice. The farmer keeps some for seed, and some to eat, and sells the rest.

In wealthier countries, rice-growing is done with machinery. Large areas of land are levelled and flooded. Rice seeds are scattered from aeroplanes. As the crops grow they are sprayed against disease. The crop is harvested by combine harvester.

America and Australia export most of their rice. America is the world's biggest exporter. 90 per cent of all rice is grown in Asia, but Asia eats all its rice and buys more.

Maize

Until 500 years ago, maize grew only on the American continent. Now it grows on all the other continents too, but America still produces more than half the world's maize.

Maize looks quite different to wheat or rice. It has a stout, solid stem about two metres tall. The 'ear' of corn can be longer than a man's hand. It is enclosed by a hardened growth of leaves called a husk.

First the farmer ploughs and levels his field. This kills weeds, and buries the remains of last year's crop. To sow the seed he uses a machine called a row planter. The rows are made between 60 and 90 centimetres apart. The biggest machines

In Ohio a group of farmers inspect the ears of corn. The stalks are now full grown.

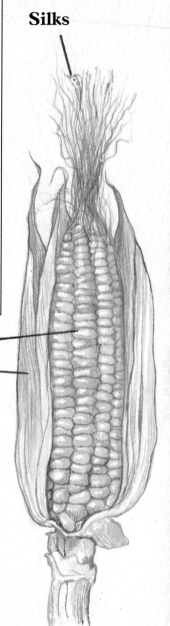

Silks

Grains

Husk

can plant twenty-four rows at a time, but four or six rows are more usual.

Maize takes between four and six months to ripen. In poor countries it is harvested by hand. The farmer simply cuts the ear off with a heavy knife. Then he chops the stalk into small pieces, so that it rots before the next planting.

The most up-to-date machine is called a corn combine. It picks the ear from the stalk, removes the husk, shells the corn, and even cleans it.

Most maize is turned into FODDER for farm animals. However, people eat it too. It is the main food in some African countries where wheat and rice cannot grow. Maize is best known to children as corn flakes, corn-on-the-cob, or popcorn. In Mexico it is used to make tortillas. It is not so good for you as wheat or rice, and it cannot be made into bread.

Corn in a Kansas field has turned golden-brown. It is time for the picker-sheller combines to start work.

Ready to Eat

Each morning, on a small rice farm, the mother grinds enough grain to last her family through the day. She pounds it in a wooden bowl with a pole, knocking off the HULLS.

Poor wheat farmers often grind their grain by another very old method. They put it between two big, round stones. Keeping the lower one still, they turn the upper one. This is called 'milling', because it is how the grain used to be ground in windmills. In several countries windmills are still used today to grind the grain.

However, most grain is grown on very large farms and sold direct to food manufacturing companies.

The biggest use of wheat is in making bread. First it is ground up into flour. When mixed with

Grain elevators tower above a Great Lakes ship locked into the ice of Toronto Harbour.

water and yeast it is called dough. When the dough is left in a warm place for about two hours the yeast makes it expand to two or three times its size.

When the dough has risen it is stirred around a bit more, then baked in a very hot oven. After about half an hour it is a delicious, crusty loaf.

Not many people make their own bread these days. It is made in large factories or local bakeries.

Breakfast cereals were first made in America

about 130 years ago. There are four main types:
Flaked Cereals. Wheat, rice, or maize is ground up, cooked with flavours or syrups, then pressed into flakes between rollers. Finally it is toasted.

Puffed Cereals. Cooked wheat or rice is 'exploded' in an oven, which expands the grain to several times its original size.

Shredded Cereals. Wheat is cooked in a pressure cooker. Then it is squeezed into long strands between heavy rollers, and shaped into slabs.

Granular Cereals. A dough of wheat and barley flour is cooked, crumbled, then baked again. Finally it is ground into rough grains, and probably coated with a sweet flavouring.

You will be able to recognize at least one each of these on the supermarket shelf. Which is your favourite – the one with the nicest taste or the one with the best free gift in the box?

Glossary

chaff: the hulls and leafy bits which cover the grains.

combine harvester: a machine which travels across a field cutting the grain, separating it from the chaff, and cleaning it, all at the same time.

crop: a plant which is grown and harvested in large quantities.

elevator: a tall building in which grain is stored.

flour: wheat (and some other cereals) which has been ground into a powdery form, used mainly to make bread.

fodder: hay and other crops used for feeding animals in winter, when grass will not grow.

graze: to graze means to eat growing grass, like cows and sheep do.

hulls: the outer covering of grains which cannot be eaten.

pasta: macaroni, spaghetti, and similar foods made from dough enriched with egg and oil.

paddy: a field in which rice is grown. The word is also used for the rice itself after it is cut but before it is processed.

Photo sources

Australian High Commission, London: page 9, and cover and page 1 (bottom centre).
Dairylea Co-operative Inc: page 17.
Ethos Ltd: page 20.
Flour Advisory Bureau: page 2, and cover and page 1 (middle left).
Japan National Tourist Organization: page 14, and cover (top centre).
Picturepoint Ltd: pages 5, 11, 18, and cover and page 1 (middle right).
Young Library Ltd: page 6.

Index

Artwork

Among the subjects illustrated are ploughing on Prince Edward Island, pages 6/7; North American wheat harvest, pages 8/9; ploughing and planting Asian paddies in south-east Asia, page 10; rice seedlings, page 11; half-grown rice in Indonesia, page 14; Indonesian rice barns where the grain is stored, page 15; Canadian street pop-corn stall, page 16; Canadian maize-stripping contest, page 18; Philippine girl pounding the daily rice supply, page 19; Greek windmill, page 20; Italian meal of corn semolina, page 21.